VASA

Important dates in the Vasa's history

1625 King Gustavus II Adolphus signs a contract with shipbuilder Henrik Hybertsson on January 16 for the building of the Vasa. Over 1,000 oaks are felled for the project.

1626 During the spring, work commences on the building of the Vasa at Skeppsgården, the naval dockyard in Stockholm. Four hundred men are employed. Casting of the bronze guns begins.

1627 Henrik Hybertsson, the shipbuilder, dies and is succeeded by Hein Jakobsson. The Vasa is launched.

1628 King Gustavus II Adolphus visits the shipyard on January 16 and inspects the Vasa. On August 10 the ship sets off on her maiden voyage, but capsizes and sinks in the harbour. Captain Söfring Hansson is imprisoned but released; no one is held responsible for the disaster. Attempts to raise the ship fall.

1658 Albreckt von Treileben is licensed to salvage the Vasa's guns.

1664 Most of the Vasa's 64 guns are raised, using a diving bell.

1683 With the raising of one more gun, the seventeenth-century diving investigations of the Vasa are thereby concluded.

1953 Anders Franzén starts searching for the Vasa in the archives, and later by means of dragging and sounding operations in Stockholm harbour.

1956 Franzén locates the Vasa off the island of Beckholmen. In September divers start exploring the ship, which lies at a depth of 32 metres.

1957 The Navy and the Neptun Salvaging Company decide to take part in the salvaging work. Divers start digging tunnels beneath the ship. Well-preserved sculptures are retrieved.

1958 One gun is found and salvaged.

1959 Thick steel cables are drawn beneath the ship and the Neptun Salvaging Company raises the Vasa into shallower water in 16 stages.

1961 On April 24 the final lift takes place. The Vasa emerges after her 333 years in the deep. Archaeologists examine all the finds. A temporary museum is built – Wasavarvet.

1962 Spraying with preservatives begins.

1963 Divers start investigating the seabed where the Vasa foundered. Over five consecutive seasons, divers search a large area. The finds include hundreds of sculptures.

1967 Diving operations at the site of the loss are concluded.

1979 Spraying of the ship is discontinued.

1986 Ten million visitors have seen the Vasa.

1987 Work starts on the building of a new Vasa Museum.

1988 The Vasa is taken on her last voyage, from Wasavarvet to the new Museum.

1990 The Vasa Museum at Galärvarvet is opened by King Carl XVI Gustaf on June 15.

1995 The lower standing rigging is back in place

2001 The Vasa is seen by its twenty millionth visitor since it was salvaged in 1961.

The stern is the most ornamented part of the Vasa. At the top, the letters G A R and S are inscribed. They stand for Gustavus Adolphus Rex Sueciae, i.e. Gustavus Adolphus, King of Sweden. Above the letters is a bust of the young king, with two griffins holding the crown above his head.

The upper part of the stern also bears the national Swedish coat of arms, measuring two metres high and 3.25 metres wide. It is carved out of oak and comprises 22 parts. The artist was the Vasa's master-carver Mårten Redtmer.

The Vasa Catalogue was printed in Sabon
Copyright: Vasa Museum and the author
Author: Erling Matz
Photographer: Hans Hammarskiöld
plus photographs from the Museum's archives
Editor: Katarina Villner, Vasa Museum
Translation by Interverbum
Layout: Christer Jonson
Printing: Davidsons Tryckeri AB 2012
Paper: Munken Lynx

ISBN 978-91-976923-9-7

«Between four and five o'clock, the great new warship Vasa keeled over and sank.» A few short lines about a major disaster were written in this book on August 10, 1628. For a magnificent ship that sank on her very first voyage, this could have been the end. Instead, it was the beginning of an adventure that is still in progress. The Vasa was found almost intact, standing on the seabed, after three centuries. The ship was salvaged and is now one of the foremost tourist attractions in the world.

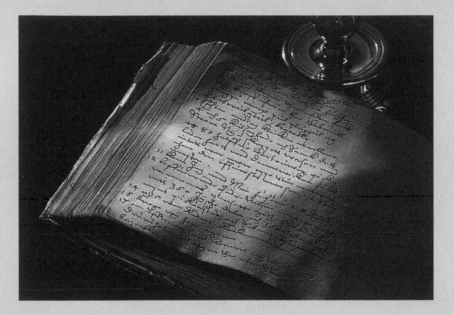

The Vasa was the most expensive and richly ornamented naval vessel built in Sweden at this time. When the Vasa sailed forth on her maiden voyage, Stockholmers stood along the shore to wish her good luck. They were eyewitnesses to the disaster. The Vasa capsized and sank inside Stockholm harbour.

The disaster

Drawing by Björn Landström.

STOCKHOLM, SUMMER 1628. For three years, carpenters, pit-sawyers, smiths, ropemakers, glaziers, sailmakers, painters, boxmakers, woodcarvers and other specialists had worked on building the Navy's new warship – the Vasa. She was a "royal ship", the seventeenth-century designation for the largest type of naval vessel. The Vasa was designed to be the foremost of Sweden's war-ships, with a hull constructed from one thousand oaks, 64 large guns, masts more than fifty metres high and many hundred gilded and painted sculptures. The shipyard where the Vasa was built, Skeppsgården,

was located on the island of Blasieholmen in the middle of Stockholm. In 1628 the Vasa was moored immediately below the Royal Castle. There, ballast was loaded, as well as the ammunition and guns required for the maiden voyage.

The new ship aroused the admiration and pride of Stockholmers, but intimidated the country's enemies. We know that her construction was followed with interest abroad. One good source of information on the Vasa's guns, for example, is a letter written by Erik Krabbe, the Danish Ambassador in Stockholm. Impressed, he reported that the

3

King Gustavus II Adolphus: a contemporary portrait.
National Portrait Collection at Gripsholm.
Photograph: National Art Museums.

Vasa had 48 big guns for 24-pound ammunition, eight 3-pounders, two 1-pounders and six mortars.

By Sunday August 10, everything was ready for the maiden voyage. The weather was fine and the wind light. On board were around a hundred crew members, but also women and children. This was to be a great ceremonial occasion, with pomp and circumstance, so the crew had been given permission to take their families on the first voyage out through the archipelago.

Countless curious spectators gathered in the harbour. They had plenty of time to follow the ship's departure. The wind was from the south-west and, for the first few hundred metres, the Vasa had to be pulled along using anchors. At Tranbodarna, the present-day Slussen, Captain Söfring Hansson issued the order: "Set the foresail, foretop, maintop and mizzen! "

The sailors climbed the rig and set four of the Vasa's ten sails. The guns fired a salute and slowly, serenely, the Vasa set off on her first voyage.

In a letter to the King, the Council of the Realm described the subsequent course of events: "When the ship left the shelter of Tegelviken, a stronger wind entered the sails and she immediately began to heel over hard to the lee side; she righted herself slightly again until she approached Beckholmen,

where she heeled right over and water gushed in through the gun ports until she slowly went to the bottom under sail, pennants and all."

Struck by a powerful gust of wind, the Vasa capsized and sank after a voyage of only 1,300 metres.

Admiral Erik Jönsson witnessed to the terrifying seconds on board when water poured in through the gun ports and the ship began to sink. Jönsson was inside the ship, checking the guns: "By the time I came up from the lower deck, the water had risen so high that the staircase had come loose and it was only with great difficulty that I climbed out."

The Admiral became "so waterlogged and badly knocked about by the hatches" that he was near death for several days. Some fifty people are said to have followed the Vasa into the deep.

News of the disaster did not reach the Swedish King, who was then in Prussia, until two weeks later. He wrote to the Council of the Realm in Stockholm that "imprudence and negligence" must have been the cause, and that the guilty parties must be punished.

1. This is where the Vasa was built. 2. In the early summer of 1628, the Vasa was moved to the quay below the Royal Castle. There, guns, ballast and equipment were taken on board. 3. On August 10 1628, the Vasa was kedged to Tranbodarna (present-day Slussen), and set sail, 4. The Vasa's route. 5. After 1,300 metres, at Tegelviken, the wind increased and the Vasa capsized and sank 100 metres off the island of Beckholmen.

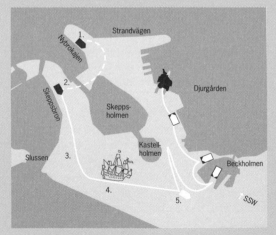

Why did the Vasa sink?

The Vasa was built here at Skeppsgården, which was situated on the island of Blasieholmen, Stockholm, opposite the Royal Castle. Four hundred men worked there. Drawing by Björn Landström.

WERE YOU INTOXICATED? Had you failed to secure the guns properly? Questions and accusations echoed in the hall at the Royal Castle. Just twelve hours after the loss of the Vasa her Danish-born Captain, Söfring Hansson, stood before the Council of the Realm. He had been taken prisoner immediately afterwards, and the report on his interrogation has survived to this day.

"You can cut me in a thousand pieces if all the guns were not secured," he answered. "And before God Almighty I swear that no one on board was intoxicated."

Söfring Hansson thus swore that he was innocent.

"It was just a small gust of wind, a mere breeze, that overturned the ship," Söfring Hansson went on to relate. "The ship was too unsteady, although all the ballast was on board."

Thus, Söfring Hansson placed the blame on the ship's design – and, by the same token, the shipbuilder.

When the crew were later questioned, they said the same thing. No mistake was made on board. It was impossible to load more ballast. The guns were properly lashed down. It was a Sunday, many people had been to Communion and no member of the crew was drunk. Instead, the fault lay in the unstable construction of the ship: the keel was too small in relation to the hull, the rig and the artillery.

"The ship is top-heavy with her masts

5

One thousand oaks were used in building the Vasa. To meet the Navy

In order to obtain the correct dimensions, the oaks often had to be specially felled for each ship. This was one way of using a tree to obtain the right parts.

and yards, sails and guns," they declared.

Shipmaster Jöran Matsson also revealed that the Vasa's stability had been tested before the sailing. Thirty men had run back and forth across the Vasa's deck when she was moored at the quay. After three runs, they had to stop – otherwise, the Vasa would have capsized. Present during the test was Admiral Klas Fleming, one of the most influential men in the Navy. The Admiral's only comment, according to Jöran Matsson, was: If only His Majesty were at home!"

Those responsible for Skeppsgården, where the Vasa was built, were then questioned. These were shipbuilder Hein Jakobsson and Arent de Groot, the lessee of Skeppsgården. One complication was that the actual builder of the Vasa, the Dutchman Henrik Hybertsson, had died the year be-

ubstantial requirements, these valuable trees were protected by law.

fore. However, Jakobsson and de Groot also swore their innocence. The Vasa conformed to the dimensions approved by the King himself, they said. On board were a number of guns, as specified in the contract.

"Whose fault is it, then?" asked the interrogator.

"Only God knows," answered de Groot.

God and the King, both equally infallible, were thus drawn into the case. The subsequent deliberations of the Council of the Realm on the issue of guilt are unknown to us. No guilty part was ever identified, and no one was punished for the disaster.

Can we today, 380 years later, identify a guilty party and explain why the Vasa sank?

First and foremost, we can dismiss the accusation that the guns were not properly secured. When the Vasa was salvaged in

Modern archaeologists, 333 years after the disaster, were able to confirm that the ballast was densely packed into the Vasa's hold.

A carpenter's tool chest and tools were found on board the Vasa. Of the iron, only lumps of rust remained, but the handles and shapes of the breast-drills, mallets and planes look entirely modern.

1961, the gun carriages were still arrayed in neat rows, and the ropes were in place around the carriages' wheel axles. Present-day technical calculations have also shown that the Vasa is extremely top-heavy, and requires only a moderate wind force to overturn her. Thus, "a small gust of wind", as the captain said during the interrogation, was enough.

Who, then, was at fault?

• Admiral Fleming? Partly. He failed to prevent the ship's departure after the stability test, although it was within his power to do so. On the other hand, the Vasa had already been completed and the King was waiting impatiently in Prussia.

• King Gustavus II Adolphus? Partly. He was anxious to acquire a ship with as many guns as possible on board. He had also approved the ship's dimensions and was keen to have her completed rapidly.

• The shipbuilder? Partly. On the other hand, Henrik Hybertsson was a very experienced Dutch shipbuilder. He had previously built many good ships. The Vasa is extremely well constructed, and her shape does not differ from other naval vessels that sailed in the seventeenth century. All ships carrying many guns were very tall and highly unstable. It was therefore impossible to *see* that the Vasa was top-heavy.

Instead, the reason for the disaster must be sought in the defective theoretical know-how of the period. Seventeenth-century shipbuilders were incapable of making construction drawings or mathematical calculations of stability. The only recourse of the shipbuilder was to a table of figures, the ship's reckoning, which recorded certain ship measurements. The reckoning was often a well-kept secret – something a father passed on to his son. Thus, a new ship was often modelled on its predecessor.

Bur this ship was different. The Vasa was more massive, and had more heavy guns, than previous ships. The great, beautiful warship was *too* large and *too* strong; as a result, she was an experiment. It was not uncommon in olden days – nor, as we know, today – for bold innovations to fail.

A whole series of misfortunes hit the Swedish Navy in the 1620s; in four years, 15 of its largest vessels were lost.

Years of misfortune

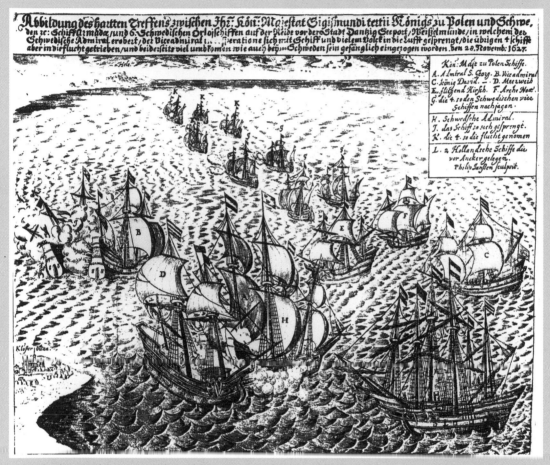

Sweden lost two large ships, *Solen* and *Tigern*, in a sea battle outside Danzig in 1627. Contemporary engraving.

"SECOND TO GOD, the welfare of the Kingdom depends on its Navy." The words were spoken by King Gustavus II Adolphus, who was well aware of the great importance of the Navy to Sweden. The King was also heavily involved in building up the Navy, and gave it four main tasks in the 1620s:

1. It was to protect Sweden against attacks from abroad.

2. It was to carry troops and material to theatres of war on the other side of the Baltic.

3. It was to provide revenue for Sweden by blocking Danzig and other ports in Poland, and by levying customs duties on the cargo ships that used them.

4. It was to blockade hostile ports, preventing the enemy's fleet from leaving, on penalty of being conquered, bombarded or sunk.

9

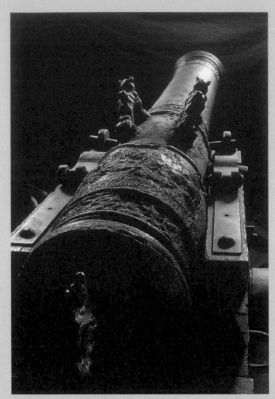

One of the Vasa's large, 24-pounder bronze guns.

1628. Within less than a month, Sweden lost three large vessels. The Vasa capsized and sank in Stockholm. Admiral Klas Fleming's flagship *Kristina* collided with another Swedish ship during a storm in the Gulf of Danzig. The flagship went out of control, drifted ashore and was wrecked. At Viksten in the southern Stockholm archipelago, *Riksnyckeln* went aground and sank.

Northern Europe, 1628. Down on the Continent, the war was raging that was to last for thirty years. On one side were the German Catholics, led by the Emperor; on the other were the Protestant states.

King Gustavus II Adolphus was, however, not yet prepared in 1628 to enter the war on the Protestant side. Since 1621, Sweden had been at war with Poland, where the Catholic Sigismund, Gustavus Adolphus' cousin, was king. Sigismund, who bad been deposed from the Swedish throne in 1599, was still making claims to be reinstated as king.

The primary theatres of war were Polish Livonia and Polish Prussia. The Swedes were highly successful, and a ceasefire was concluded in autumn 1629. In the following year, Gustavus Adolphus entered the major European war on the Protestant side. In June 1630, the Swedish army gathered at Älvsnabben in the southern Stockholm archipelago. From there, the King sailed to Germany on June 17, with 15,000 men on board 37 ships. They disembarked on the German island of Usedom on Midsummer Day.

A large, strong navy was essential to perform these tasks. The many accidents that befell Swedish vessels in the 1620s were therefore serious. In four years, Sweden lost 15 of its largest warships.

1625. In this year – the year in which the Vasa was ordered – the Swedish Navy was surprised by a storm while cruising in the Bay of Riga, and ten ships went aground and were wrecked.

1627. A Swedish and a Polish fleet clashed off the Polish coast. The Swedish flagship *Tigern* was captured, and *Solen* was blown up by her own crew in order to avoid the same fate.

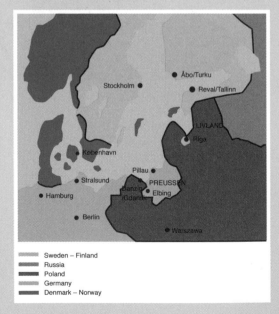

Sweden – Finland
Russia
Poland
Germany
Denmark – Norway

"Men who can walk under water" was the appellation for divers in the seventeenth century. They succeeded in bringing up most of the Vasa's guns.

Salvage attempts in the seventeenth century

WHILE CAPTAIN SÖFRING Hansson was still in captivity, the first wreck salvagers arrived at the site of the shipwreck. The Englishman Ian Bulmer was the first to arrive; only three days after the disaster, he was given the sole right of salvaging the Vasa. But the wise Councillors of the Realm stipulated that no money would be paid until Bulmer had fulfilled his promises.

Bulmer failed, and Admiral Klas Fleming – the same man who interrupted the stability test – took over attempts to salvage the Vasa and save the many valuable guns. To assist him, he engaged Hans Olofsson from Karelia, who "could walk under water". But Olofsson failed as well, and after a year of fruitless attempts Fleming wrote to the King: "This is a more onerous task than I could ever have foreseen."

Fleming gave up, but many others were attracted by the valuable Vasa guns. In the decades after the shipwreck, numerous adventurers, treasure-seekers and inventors arrived in Stockholm. Hooks and anchors were fastened to the hull; they pulled and tugged, but all to no avail. The treasures of the Vasa remained inaccessible right up to the 1660s, when Albreckt von Treileben, the Swede from Värmland, and the German Andreas Peckell began to take an interest in the 64 guns. Both men had extensive experience of salvaging wrecks, and their primary tool was a diving bell. This worked in the same way as if one places an upside-down glass in water: a pocket of air formed in the upper part of the diving bell. This was the diver's air supply, while he worked down on the wreck with hooks and special tools. The first diver to be lowered to the Vasa was called Anders Amundsson. He reported that the previous salvagers had caused considerable damage to the ship: "It looks like a makeshift fence down there," he said.

The Italian Gerolamo Cardano, like the Swede Olaus Magnus, demonstrated how ships could be salvaged in the mid-sixteenth century. The technique used in salvaging the Vasa in 1961 was basically the same.

In the seventeenth century, Sweden was a leading country when it came to diving and salvage work. The illustration is of a diving-bell, as depicted in Francesco Negri's book *Viaggio settentrionale*. Negri witnessed the salvaging of the Vasa's guns in the 1660s

Under the leadership of von Treileben and Peckell, the salvage work commenced. In pitch-darkness, at a depth of thirty metres, the divers were to (1) loosen the guns, weighing one ton each, from their carriages; (2) remove the guns through the gun ports; and (3) bring the guns up to the surface. They succeeded: over fifty guns were lifted during the years 1664 and 1665.

An eyewitness account of the salvage operations has survived. Francesco Negri, an Italian priest who was on a short visit to Stockholm, observed the diving operations of 1663. He wrote in his diary: "The diver was entirely clad in leather and had double leather boots. He stood on a platform of lead hanging under the diving bell.

"I asked him how long he could stay down there on the seabed. He answered 'Half an hour'. But this was at the end of October, and after quarter of an hour the bell was hoisted up, and the man was then shivering with cold although he was a strong, native Swede.

"I myself wanted to try the diving bell, but was advised to refrain since the water was so cold and there was a danger of falling ill in consequence."

The achievement of the "men who could walk under water" was a remarkable one. These heroes included Abraham Eriksson, Anders Dykare, Johan Printz, Johan Bertilsson, Johan Wik and Lars Andersson, all from Gothenburg. By way of comparison, it may be mentioned that, in the 1950s, it took a whole day for a deep-sea diver with modern equipment to salvage one of the Vasa's remaining guns.

This is how the real thing must have looked.
A copy of Teileben's diving bell was made and tested in 1960.

Anders Franzén, who discovered the Vasa. A piece of blackened oak fastened in the hollow punch of the sampler. This was the core sampler with which Franzén found the Vasa in August 1956.

The Baltic is a unique source of treasure trove. In the brackish water, wooden vessels are preserved for centuries. One of them was the Vasa. But where was the old warship?

Discovery and salvaging

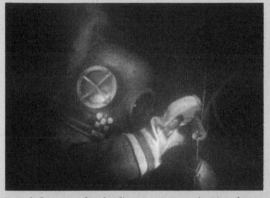
It took five years for the divers to prepare the Vasa for the arduous salvaging operation.

O N SEPTEMBER 13 1956, a notice in *Expressen*, the evening paper, announced: "An old ship has been found off Beckholmen in the middle of Stockholm. It is probably the warship Vasa, which sank on her maiden voyage in 1628. For five years, a private person has been engaged in a search for the ship."

It was a short notice about a major sensation. The "private person" was the 38-year-old engineer Anders Franzén. He was, in fact, one of Sweden's foremost experts on naval warfare in the sixteenth and seventeenth centuries and a specialist on wrecked naval vessels. He was also one of the few who both researched in archives and then went out on a boat to find the site of the wreck.

Franzén knew that the Baltic is unique. Here there is no shipworm, the tiny *Teredo* that destroys all wood in saltier seas. Wooden vessels that sink in the Baltic are therefore preserved for centuries, indeed millennia.

Franzén relates that it was Professor Nils Ahnlund, an eminent authority on seventeenth-century Sweden, who first aroused his interest in the Vasa.

However, Professor Ahnlund did not know exactly where the Vasa had foundered, since the data in the seventeenth-century archives point to several different places. Franzén therefore set out to search the seabed of Stockholm harbour for the Vasa, with a grapnel, a sounding line, maps and information from the archives.

"My booty consisted mainly of rusty iron cookers, ladies' bicycles, Christmas trees and dead cats," Franzén relates.

After searching for several years, Franzén succeeded on August 25 1956. His home-made core sampler, with its hollow punch at the tip, got stuck and came up containing a plug of blackened oak. A few days later, the diver Per Edvin Fälting went down and was able to confirm Franzén's find. Over a crackling diver's telephone, he reported: 'I can't see anything, since it's pitch-dark here, but I can feel something big – the side of a ship. Here's one gun port and here's another.

The shipworm, *Teredo*, rapidly devours and destroys all wood. But this tiny marine clam does not occur in the Baltic, which is insufficiently saline. This is why sunken wooden ships may be preserved for centuries.

The Vasa pioneers were the first people to board the Vasa. Discoverer Anders Franzén (right) and chief diver Per Edvin Fälting (left).

There are two rows. It must be the Vasa"

Anders Franzén and Per Edvin Fälting then became two of the main protagonists in the Vasa adventure. Franzén, the discoverer, devoted all his strength and powers of persuasion to saving the ship and lifting her to the surface. Fälting, the diver – who, since the Vasa had been found, had spent one-and a-half years or 12,000 hours under water – was the self-evident leader of the diving team.

Bur how was the salvaging to be done? Such a large and old ship bad never been raised before. There were numerous imaginative proposals. One was to freeze the Vasa into an immense block of ice and let her float to the surface. The idea was then to tow the iceberg to a suitable position and let it melt in the sun, whereupon the Vasa would emerge.

Another suggestion was to fill the Vasa with table-tennis balls: when enough had been placed inside, the ship would rise to the surface of her own accord.

After 333 years, the Vasa broke the surface on the morning of 24 April 1961.
The press, radio and TV from the whole world followed this unique event.

However, the Neptun Salvaging Company, an experienced Swedish enterprise, considered that a conventional technique was best.
Heavy cables were to be laid beneath the hull and attached to water-filled pontoons. When the water was pumped out of the pontoons they would rise, stretching the cables and lifting the Vasa from the seabed. Broströms, the parent company of the Neptun Salvaging Company, also promised to carry out the work free of charge.

A large, nationwide "Save the Vasa" campaign was launched, and money and materials were donated by foundations, individuals and companies. The Navy made staff and boats available, and in autumn 1957 the divers began to dig, or rather flush out, tunnels beneath the ship. Their tool was a hosepipe with a special mouthpiece. Mud and gravel were washed away – a task requiring immense technical skill and even greater courage. The work was carried out at a depth of more than thirty metres and in

About fifty people drowned when the Vasa sank, according to a contemporary report. Twenty-five skeletons were found in or near the ship.
Photograph: Anders Franzén,

The Vasa was so well preserved that, after being salvaged, she was able to float unaided.

total darkness. The tunnels were so narrow that the divers had to squirm through. Girders, plans and other paraphernalia meant that the air pipes and lines could easily get stuck – and they often did. Above their heads, the divers also had a 300-year-old ship weighing over a thousand tons, with a ballast of stones in the hold. No one could be sure that the Vasa would stand the strain.

Chief diver Per Edvin Fälting's advice to the divers who were going down for the first time was: "If it feels as if you're expiring down there in the darkness and cold, just don't give a damn and find out what you've done wrong!"

Work on the tunnels went on for two years, and no serious accident occurred.

At the end of August 1959 it was time for the first lift. The Neptun Salvaging Company's salvaging pontoons were placed above the Vasa, cables were pulled through the six tunnels and the old ship was raised from the seabed without any problems. The hull did not give way, and the Vasa was then lifted into shallower water in 16 stages. It was still too early to bring the Vasa up to the surface. The hull had to be made watertight and reinforced for the final lift. Again, it was the divers who performed this task. For two years they were busy filling the thousands of holes formed where iron bolts had rusted away. The partially broken stern had to be reconstructed and all the gun ports fitted with new, watertight hatches.

The Vasa's first resting-place after the salvaging was a dry dock at Beckholmen, immediately adjacent to the place where she sank. Here, for the first time, the royal warship could be seen in her entirety.

On April 24 1961, everything was ready for the lift. Newspapers, radio and TV teams from all over the world were in position. After 333 years on the seabed, the Vasa broke the surface and a piece of untouched seventeenth-century history came to light. When the railing was above the surface, powerful bilge pumps were started. By May 4 the ship was so free of water and mud that she was able to float and be towed into a dock at Beckholmen. The first people on board the Vasa were, of course, the pioneers Anders Franzén and Per Edvin Fälting.

Archaeological excavations

The archaeologists were able to enter an untouched relic from the seventeenth century.
But it was cramped, dirty and damp.

On the bottom deck of the Vasa, the mud was a metre thick – a black sludge, full of finds and, perhaps, bacteria. After being vaccinated against tetanus, typhus, jaundice and other infectious diseases, the archaeologists climbed on board.

A sunken ship is a unique treasure trove. Senior archaeologist Per Lundström and his rubber-clad men were able to walk, crawl, squirm and wade straight into the early seventeenth century. Following traditional archaeological practice, all the finds were described and numbered. The site of each find, in particular, was important. What was found in the stern of the ship presumably belonged to the captain and senior officers. The finds on the battery deck were presumably the seamen's possessions.

In the first fortnight 3,000 finds were registered, and by the time the excavation on board was completed five months later, 14,000 finds had been registered.

When the Vasa was salvaged, everyone thought it was a remarkably well-preserved ship. But more than three centuries on the seabed had also wrought a great deal of destruction.

World's largest jigsaw puzzle

The Swedish national emblem was pieced together by the Vasa carpenters. It comprised 22 parts and was meant to be attached to the stern.

MANY PEOPLE PULLED and toiled on the old ship. Nearly 40 large anchors dating from different centuries were in position on the Vasa when she was salvaged. Admittedly, the hull was intact, but most of the stern was crushed, as was the beak-head in the foreship, and also the upper deck.

Fitting together the more than 13,500 fragments was a task for the museum's scientists and a team of carpenters led by Johan Blomman. There were no construction drawings when the Vasa was built. The carpenters' primary tools were therefore their own imagination and some thick steel wire. The steel wire was pushed through the old nail-holes on the pieces that had come loose. If the holes fitted the marks and holes on the ship, a new piece of the jigsaw had been found.

Since 1961, the Vasa has gradually been restored in her entirety. The ship is 95% original. At the same time, no one need wonder what is original and what is new. Newly manufactured parts have retained their smooth surface and differ markedly from the Vasa's dark, rough oak.

Another result of the restoration is that now, for the first time in the world, there are complete drawings of a seventeenth-century ship. This is both useful and gratifying to researchers, model-builders and other interested parties.

The hull was sprayed for many years with preservative to prevent it from cracking.
During this time, there was a thick mist in the temporary museum building.

The brackish, deoxygenated water and mud on the seabed had saved the Vasa. After the salvaging, the hazards were considerably greater.

Preservation

WATERLOGGED WOOD STARTS splitting and shrinking after only a few days in warm, dry air. The Vasa would crack apart unless the wood was preserved. But how is one to preserve 1,080 tonnes of waterlogged oak with a volume of 900 sqm. In addition, there were 13,500 wooden components of various sizes, 500 figure sculptures and 200 ornaments, plus 12,000 small objects made of wood, textiles, leather and metal.

There was no previous experience of preserving such a large volume of waterlogged wood. The method adopted was spraying with a mixture of water and polyethylene glycol (PEG), a substance used in such products as lipstick and hand cream. PEG has the capacity to penetrate wood and displace water, thus preventing shrinkage and cracking.

Large quantities of water had to be removed. When the Vasa came to the surface, each kilo of dry wood contained 1.5 kg of water; 1.35 kg had to be removed, i.e. a total of 580 tonnes from the whole ship.

Sculptures and small wooden details were treated in vats filled with PEG solution – a method that, for obvious reasons, could not be used for the entire hull. The hull of the Vasa was sprayed with a solution of PEG in water instead. The spraying was commenced in 1962, and from then on it was misty in the temporary museum building. For 25 minutes, the solution was sprayed from 500 mouthpieces, and after 20 minutes' interval spraying was recommenced for another 25 minutes –and so on, 24 hours a day. Visitors to the Vasa in these years remember the humidity and the great black dripping hull looming in the mist.

The preservation of the Vasa is a labour that never ends. New challenges and problems are always arising. In 2000, for instance, it was discovered that the preserved wood was beginning to exude sulphur here and there. The sulphur had penetrated into the wood during the Vasa's 300 years at the bottom of Stockholm harbour. A programme of research to deal with this problem is engaging experts from all over the world. The goal is always the same: to ensure that the Vasa is preserved for future generations.

Clothes and shoes from those who died on the Vasa were carefully preserved.

When it solidifies, the preservative polyethylene glycol has roughly the same consistency as candlewax. Here, the surplus has formed a stalactite cave around the Vasa's small wooden vessels.

Six of the Vasa's ten sails were found during the excavations. They were so large that they could not bear their own weight. All the work on the sails therefore had to be carried out under water. The sails were unfolded, cleaned and dried with alcohol and xylene. They were then mounted on a supportive web of glass fibre. In this way, 170 m² of sails were saved.

The Vasa's sails, fore to aft: 1. spritsail, 2. upper spritsail, 3. fore topgallant, 4. fore topsail, 5. foresail, 6. main topgallant, 7. main topsail, 8. mainsail, 9. mizzen topsail, 10. mizzen.

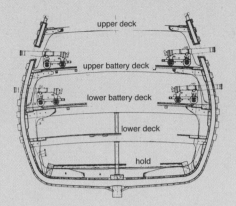

Vasa in figures

LENGTH
The total length of the Vasa, including bowsprit, is 69 metres. The hull, between the prow and the stern, is 47.5 metres long.

WIDTH
Maximum width: 11.7 metres.

HEIGHT
From keel to the top of the main mast: 52.5 metres. Height of the stern: 19.3 metres.

DRAUGHT
4.8 metres.

DISPLACEMENT
1,210 tons.

SAIL AREA
1,275 m .

NO. OF SAILS
Ten (of which six have been preserved).

ARMAMENT
64 guns, including 48 24-pounders, eight 3-pounders, two 1-pounders and six mortars.

CREW
145 seamen.
300 soldiers (not on board when the Vasa sank).

What the Vasa tells us

Time stopped on the Vasa at five o'clock on 10 August 1628. When the ship was salvaged 333 years later, the seamen's chests were still packed with provisions, clothes and small personal possessions. Barrels of meat lay in the hold, the admiral's table stood in the cabin, the officers' beautiful pewter dinner service, bronze candlesticks, lamps – and the ship's cat – were all on board. The Vasa is a time machine that witnesses to life on board ship and on land in the early 17th century, and to events on that peaceful, beautiful Sunday in August 1628.

28

The Vasa was built to impress – not only with her guns,
but also with her abundant sculptures.

Art treasures

A ROARING, grimacing lion's head was the first find brought to the surface from the Vasa. Black from its centuries in the deep, it still bore traces of golden-brown paint on the mane and red on the jaws.

The lion was subsequently to be joined by angels, devils, warriors, musicians, emperors and gods. A total of five hundred figure sculptures and more than two hundred carved ornaments decorated the Vasa.

The first lion to be found was one of the many designed to stand on the gunports. But there were several brave and strong lions on board. The most magnificent of all the Vasa lions is the one located furthest out on the beak-head at the prow of the ship: over three metres long and with its body raised to leap, it is permanently poised to fight. In the decoration, the lion symbolises the King and Sweden's strength in the struggle against the Catholics and the German Emperor. Gustavus II Adolphus was known among contemporaries as the "Lion of the North".

Most of the Vasa's sculptures have a symbolic meaning. The artists employed in the wood-carving workshop of Skeppsgården were well-versed in the complex symbolic language of the time. They found motifs and ideas in Renaissance manuals on art.

Their artistic style was German-Dutch late Renaissance and early Baroque, and there were both Dutchmen and Germans among the artists. They carved in oak, pine and lime.

The most eminent of the Vasa carvers was the German Mårten Redtmer. His work includes most of the large, expressive sculptures, including those of Hercules. There are two versions of him. As a young man he symbolises strength and courage, in his old age wisdom. Contemporaries equated the hero with King Gustavus Adolphus – the powerful warrior and wise statesman.

The Hercules motif was taken from Greek mythology. Others came from the Bible, Roman history and the legendary lineage of the Swedish royal family. The army marching across the Vasa's upper gallery in the stern, for example, is derived from the Book of Judges in the Old Testament. The men represent 23 of Gideon's warriors who, bearing torches and oil lamps in their hands and blowing trumpets and horns, are setting off to fight for their God against the Midianites.

The Vasa's beak-head bears carvings of 20 Roman emperors on parade. In seventeenth-century eyes, they were the proud forerunners of the Swedish monarch. Gustavus Adolphus regarded himself as their equal. But contemporary artists also loved coarse, bombastic, erotic and burlesque motifs. There is therefore a singular collection of curvaceous mermaids, bearded tritons and grimacing devils on display in the Vasa. A vulgar, large-breasted woman sticks her tongue out and licks her own nose, while a buxom daughter of Neptune, the sea god, stretches voluptuously and a Roman pensively twists his beard.

There is no ship's name in letters on the Vasa, but the arms of the Vasas, the Swedish royal family, exists in three versions. The coat of arms represents a sheaf of corn – a vase – and this is how the ship got her name.

The newly-built vessel was ablaze with colour. Sculptures and decorations were painted in red, green, yellow, blue and violet.

The richly coloured ship

Detail of copy of sculpture in reconstructed colour.
Photo: Kristian Löveborg

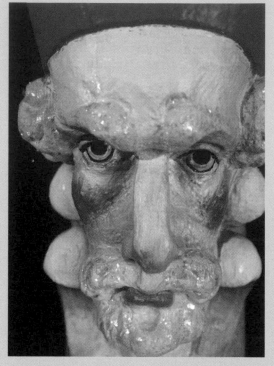

A sea creature in a biretta (a cap worn by the Catholic clergy). A copy of a sculpture from the Vasa in reconstructed colour. Photo: Stefan Evensen

EXTRAVAGANCE WAS THE fashion in seventeenth century Sweden. Life in the palaces, the manor houses and the dwellings of well-to-do burghers was a riot of food, drink, fine clothes, feasting and colour. All this brilliance and splendour proclaimed, "We have power! We have money!"

The most conspicuous example from the 1620s is the Vasa. The ship that was completed in the summer of 1628 looked very different from what we see today. The onlooker would have been overawed not only by its mighty cannon but by its hundreds of sculpted figures, and the newly-built Vasa was ablaze with colour.

Chubby angels with red cheeks, golden hair and pink round tummies jostled mermaids with rosy breasts and deep pink tails. A Roman warrior stood on guard in a cloak of red and yellow flames, while the royal coat of arms was hung with blue grapes, oranges and lemons.

The hundreds of sculptures clinging and clambering about the Vasa were an orgy of pink naked flesh, of steel-blue armour, of sanguine reds, poisonous greens and marine blues.

Today we might well dismiss it all as so much vulgarity. In the seventeenth century they called it peerless and were willingly impressed.

So how do we know what the Vasa

The Vasa's stern in reconstructed colour. Painting by Göte Göransson.

looked like when it was new? How can we be sure that the dark, austere ship we see today was not that of the 1600s?

The quest for the colours has been led by scientists, who have searched the Vasa's sculptures under their microscopes for fragments of paint. Analysing hundreds of samples from each sculpture, they have identified pigments including copper blue,

iron red, and lead white. We know, too, that the Skeppsgården shipyards shipyard, where the Vasa was built, bought twenty or so different kinds of pigment. Painted wooden sculptures in churches and palaces provide valuable parallels. There too we find pink-cheeked angels and other brightly-painted mythological figures. But nowhere else are there so many as on the Vasa.

31

32   One chest contained a hat, clothes and other belongings, still neatly packed when the chest was opened after the salvaging.

The crew

THE SWEDES ARE NO worse seamen than the Dutch, as long as they get proper wages and are treated well, King Gustavus Adolphus once wrote in an official letter.

In a letter to the same King, Admiral Klas Fleming complained that the lamentable wages meant that the fleet was manned with vagrants. He continued in the same bitter vein, remarking that the best seamen defected to foreign fleets where wages were better.

In the Vasa's day, the fleet was largely manned by conscription. One man in ten was usually taken on active service. Children under 15 and old men over 60 were exempt. In addition, a system of maritime inscription was tried out in towns and parishes along the coast. It was a counterpart to the military tenure-establishment system of a later period.

Both conscription and maritime inscription had major shortcomings, however, and a large number of people were needed. In 1628, the year in which the Vasa was to be taken into operation, the problem was particularly acute. When the fleet had arrived in Stockholm the previous autumn, the seamen were forced to stay in the capital. Otherwise, they were usually permitted to go home. The reason was the fear that the ships would lack crews when they went out to sea again in the spring. The burghers of Stockholm had to provide board and lodging, according to the Council of the Realm's resolution. There is no information in the archives on what the seamen thought, but the burghers complained about the extra tax levied, writing that they could pay it "only with tears and considerable hardship".

What, then, did an ordinary seaman receive in wages? In 1628, annual wages amounted to 57 dalers. Food on board and material for clothes were deducted from this sum, and he received barely one-quarter in cash. What could he buy? At that time, for

Four thousand coins were found on board the Vasa. Most of them, were made of copper.

example, a cow cost 5 dalers, a goose half a daler, a barrel of rye 1 daler and a barrel of beer 3 dalers.

By way of comparison, it may be mentioned that a captain's salary was 475 dalers, while a lieutenant received 260, a trumpeter 114 and a cabin boy 38.

Planned composition of the Vasa's crew

SEAMEN	
1 admiral	20 gunners
1 medical orderly *(barber)*	1 cook
1 priest	1 cook's assistant
1 trumpeter	4 cabin boys
1 captain	4 carpenters
2 lieutenants	1 flog-master
2 steersmen	
2 shipmasters	SOLDIERS
1 leading seaman *(chief gunner)*	Two companies,
12 deck officers	comprising
90 seamen	30 commanding officers
	270 men

This is how a seaman was attired in 1628: in a short jacket, sometimes with a standing collar, and kneelength breeches shirred at the waist and wide over the thighs. Under the jacket he wore a woven linen shirt, and on his feet sewn socks and soft leather shoes or boots. There was no standard uniform.

Part of his wages went on fabric. A seaman's outfit required some six metres. The fabric cost 6 daler, or one-tenth of a seaman's annual wages.

The clothes had to be warm and hard-wearing, since the poor seamen often had no others. The ships were out at sea late in the autumn and there was no heating on board. The home-spun clothes were the seaman's only protection against damp and cold. Sewing, patching and mending were therefore an important part of life on board. Sewing accessories have been found in the crew's chests, as have leather, lasts and shoe pegs for repairing shoes.

Gloves and shoes were simple. They may have been made by the owner himself.

Life on board

A small box bearing the owner's insignia on the lid contained such items as a comb, a thimble, sewing thread and wax.

HE HAD 20 1/2 öre in copper coins in his pocket when he was trapped under a gun carriage and followed the Vasa down to the deep. It would have been enough for a jug of wine at an inn in the archipelago, but no more. He was dubbed the "carriage man" by the archaeologists who found him.

The man was probably a seaman. This is indicated by the small sum of money, the clothes and his position when he died. A seaman who was not on watch or handling the sails and anchors would remain on the battery deck. There, he ate his meals, sitting on the deck or perhaps on his wooden chest; there he slept; and there he struggled for his life in battle.

There, in the semi-darkness, he lived with the other conscripts. In the Vasa's case, four hundred men would have gathered on the battery deck. The crush was enormous.

The senior officers lived in greater comfort. The captain's cabin was furnished like the state room of a palace, with gilded and finely painted sculptures on the walls, long ornamented benches and a table. Here, there were folding bunks for the admiral and his closest associates.

There is a marked difference between the simple wooden plates and spoons of the conscripts and the pewter and faience dishes used by the commanding officers. The conscripts ate in the forecastle mess, with seven men usually eating out of the same large wooden bowl. The officers ate at tables in the captain's cabin.

At the very bottom of the ship, over an open fire, the cook prepared food for the large crew.

Food and drink

Butter casks. Two of them contained 333-year-old butter.

PORRIDGE MADE OF barley groats. Grain cooked with dried beans or peas. Salt beef and pork. Dried or salt fish. Bread.

This was the monotonous diet of the crew. They ate in the semi-darkness, next to the guns, off wooden plates or earthenware bowls. As cutlery, they used their fingers, wooden spoons and sheath-knives.

They seldom, if ever, received fresh food. The result was scurvy and other deficiency diseases, as well as low resistance to illness in general.

The ship's kitchen, the galley, was right at the bottom of the ship. There, the food was cooked in a massive cast-iron cauldron over an open fire. The fireplace was made of brick. There was no chimney on the Vasa, so the smoke wafted freely up through the deck where the crew had their living quarters.

Large quantities of ale were needed to wash down the salty food. The daily ration was three litres each. Aquavit and other strong spirits were, on the other hand, scarce on board. However, several pewter flasks have been found on the Vasa, and one of them still contained spirits that, when analysed, proved to resemble rum.

As long as the ship remained in the archipelago, the crew were obliged to provide their own victuals in order to economise on the ship's provisions. Small private stores of food have also been found on board, including meat and butter.

Off duty

"I THINK THE MAIN reason why the crew fell ill is that, throughout the summer, they lay motionless on the ships and did nothing but sleep, both day and night," wrote Admiral Henrik Fleming. For long periods, nothing happened. The ships lay at anchor in the harbour or sailed to and fro on blockade duty. The crew spent their time on drills and maintenance work on the ship and their own equipment. Numerous finds from the Vasa show how the crew spent their spare time.

There are simple figures and letters carved with a knife on barrels and chests. On the lid of one barrel, someone has cut a simple parlour game for two players. One of the officers took a beautiful board game with him,

It was found in the officers' stores, at the very bottom of the stern. In one chest, there was also, a box containing a lock of hair – a cherished memento to be taken out when the yearning for a loved one grew too strong or the apprehension before a battle was unendurable.

Tobacco-smoking was a novelty in Sweden at this time. But the habit was spreading rapidly. The clay pipes found on board the Vasa are among the oldest in Sweden. As early as 1628, legislation was called for: "It is prohibited to use tobacco on board, other than in the galley," runs a proposed maritime regulation. The ban on smoking anywhere other than in the galley was, of course, prompted by the fire risk.

One officer had taken a board game with him on the Vasa, as an off-duty pastime.

Disease claimed many more victims than the enemy's guns and muskets.

Medical care

"BLOOD SICKNESS", the "shivers", ague and bone disease – contemporary illnesses had graphic names. Today, we would call them dysentery, malaria or diphtheria. The risk of dying from an epidemic on board was much greater than that of dying in battle. Non-existent hygiene, poor diet and crowded conditions on board made an excellent breeding-ground for illnesses. Axel Oxenstierna described the situation in a letter to the King as follows.

"By the time a ship has lain in the roadstead for a couple of months, half the crew has been cast overboard (i.e. buried at sea)," he reported. Sometimes things were even worse. The year 1628 was a particularly bad one: in Admiral Henrik Fleming's squadron off the Polish coast, two-thirds of the men were sick or dying or had already been "cast overboard".

"Since we sailed from Kalmar, thirty men have died and no more than seven seamen and twelve soldiers on my ship are healthy, wrote the Admiral. On board only 19 men fit for work, instead of 115, remained.

Nonetheless, Fleming was solicitous about his crew and their health. When scurvy was at its worst, Fleming got hold of 200 lemons and gave them to the sufferers – and this was 125 years before the Scotsman James Lind proved that citrus fruits cured scurvy.

The barber – the person on board with a knowledge of medical care – could do little else to help. Treatments consisted of enemas, emetics, blood-letting and herbal medicines.

The skeletons found on board the Vasa also confirm the grim truth. Several bear marks of violence and disease.

This has been interpreted as the medical equipment on board. If so, the barber - who was also the ship's surgeon - used the grater, whisk, mortar and pestle to prepare medicines from spices, herbs and spirits.

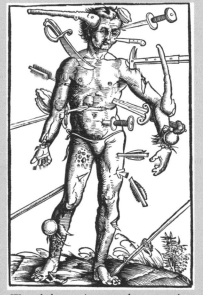

Wounded man. A copperplate engraving four hundred years old shows how a warrior might be wounded.
Hans von Gersdorff, 1517

Keel-hauling and other punishments

Even for minor offences, the sentence might be keel-hauling or running the yard.
Contemporary German copperplate engraving.

T HE CREW WERE KEPT in good order by means of threats of cruel punishments, meted out with the whole crew looking on. For picking a fight, a man had a knife stuck through his hand, "slitting it to the fingers". Those who complained about the food were put in irons and given bread and water for ten days. Anyone who started a fire was thrown into the flames. A killer was bound back to back with his victim and thrown overboard. Blasphemy or insolence to the admiral was punished by keel-hauling.

Keel-hauling was a common punishment enshrined in the ships' regulations, and sometimes it amounted to the death penalty. The condemned man was hoisted up to a yard, dropped head first into the water and pulled with a rope under the keel to the other side of the ship. Keel-hauling was carried out "once, twice or thrice according to the nature of the offence". Even if the offender did not drown, there was a considerable risk of his being so badly cut by limpets and barnacles under the ship that death followed later.

However, the extent to which these cruel forms of corporal punishment were carried out is uncertain.

Court documents contemporary with the Vasa tell us about crimes, criminals and punishments. A few examples:

• Seaman Erik Jakobsson, known as "Rat", belonged to the crew of the Äpplet. He was a hardened thief with two previous convictions. The first time he was punished by the gauntlet. The second time he was condemned to hang but was pardoned. Now he had been caught for a third time. He had stolen a cooking pot and some rags of clothing from crewmates, and at Kalmar he had attempted to desert ship. Seaman Erik Jakobsson was condemned to death and hanged.

• A leading seaman stole a plank of wood from the Naval Shipyard in Stockholm. He was condemned to be keelhauled three times and disrated to Ordinary Seaman.

• Captain Petter Petterson was berthed with his ship the Jungfrun below the Royal Palace in Stockholm. While there he ordered Leading Seaman Mats Esping to fire a salute for a Russian envoy. Mats fired so unskilfully that a butcher standing near the palace was shot in the leg and died. The court, however, acquitted Mats and instead convicted Captain Petterson, who had ordered the salute to be fired. He was condemned to forfeit one month's pay.

Naval warfare

"In order to make the young fighters fiercer and more stalwart when they encounter the enemy, they should be given two kegs of ale to drink," run the ship's regulations. In other words, in order for the crew to withstand the horrors of marine warfare and succeed in fighting, they had to be fortified with beer. Giving them extra beer rations was one of the many preparations for battle. Others included the following.

• To prevent fire breaking out on board, seamen were ordered up into the rigging to wet the sails. The battery deck was supposed to be under one decimetre of water. Wet skins were also laid in strategic places.

• Carpenters used plugs and sheet lead to seal bullet holes.

• Soldiers equipped with incendiary shells were positioned up on the masts; pikes, muskets and axes were distributed; and the barber took out his saw and knife in readiness to perform amputations.

• The soldiers took up their positions by the guns and laid in supplies of ammunition. However, gunpowder was never permitted to stand next to the guns owing to the risk of explosion. It had to be fetched from the depths of the hold after every shot.

A naval battle at the beginning of the seventeenth century usually began with an artillery duel but was then succeeded by boarding and man-to-man combat.

Loading and aiming was also a lengthy business. Before the officers gave the order to fire, many different manoeuvres were required. It was hardly possible to shoot more than ten times an hour, partly because of the time-consuming loading process and partly because of the heat in the gun-tubes.

An eyewitness account of a naval battle in 1627 exists. It describes how the Swedish ship *Tigern* was captured by the Poles, and it gives a terrifying glimpse of the slaughter

Ammunition of various kinds, as well as linstocks and gun-ladles, were found on board the Vasa. Round cannonballs were fired at ships' hulls, while pointed and rod-shaped lead bullets which spun in the air were used for shots aimed at the crew and the rigging.

Large supplies of musketshot were found in barrels on the Vasa's deck.

involved in such a battle. "A bullet hit Admiral Stiernsköld's arm, causing him to fall down immediately; he tried to get up several times, bur be was too weak. His servant Mats then had both his arm-bones shot away, so that the flesh alone remained. Then the enemy boarded the ship and cut down some of our men.

"While the enemy ravaged the ship pitiably, the poor admiral lay in the cabin, with his servant Mats sitting in a chair beside him. The admiral then asked for a priest and took communion. The barber then cut off both Mats' arms, and he immediately gave up the ghost. Poor Stiernsköld also let the barber cut off his arm. When be felt that the time was nigh be took the priest's hand in his own bloody one and passed into a sweet sleep."

During the same battle, a Swedish ship was blown to pieces, according to instructions, by its own crew. The instructions said: 'It is better for an 'honest, trustworthy Swede' to run down to the gunpowder store and set it alight than for the ship to fall into enemy hands."

Illness and combat were the greatest threats to the crew's lives, but the ships' sailing characteristics were another major hazard.

Sailing characteristics

"WE PUT OUT TO SEA if God and the wind are on our side," as Admiral of the Realm Karl Karlsson Gyllenhielm once wrote to the King.

Tacking this way and that in narrow fairways and through the small channels between the Baltic islands was also impossible. The ships were therefore often forced to remain stationary for long periods waiting for a suitable wind.

It might, accordingly, take a month to sail the short distance from Stockholm to the open sea.

Nonetheless, a ship could sail from Sweden to the ports on the other side of the Baltic in a few days if the wind was right.

Storms, foundering, capsizing and beaching were also constant threats. In the late 1620s, Sweden lost 15 naval ships – but only two in battle; the other 13 foundered owing to their limited sailing capacity.

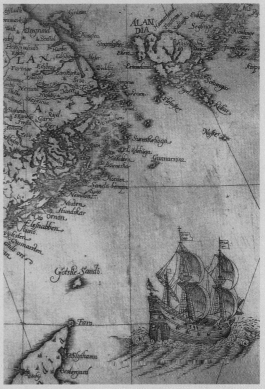

Swedish maps of the early seventeenth century were of little use for navigational purposes.
Anders Bure's map from 1626.

Sails, sail twine and lengths of rope were found on board the Vasa. Two pieces of rope was tied together with a reef knot.

A sudden wind change could make the ship start drifting towards the coast and eventually go aground. Tacking away from the shore was seldom possible for such unwieldy vessels.

*The warship Vasa now has her own
museum in the middle of Stockholm.*

The Vasa Museum

IF YOU LOOK OUT of the windows of the
Vasa Museum, you can see the site where
the Vasa was built. And it is only a few
hundred metres to the spot where the Vasa
sank. The fact that the museum also oc-
cupies the site of the former naval dockyard
conforms to the long historical tradition.

When a Nordic architectural competition
was announced before the building of the
museum, the outcome beat every record:
as many as 384 proposals were submitted.
Hidemark & Månsson Arkitektkontor AB,
later Månsson Dahlbäck Arkitektkontor AB,
was the architects' firm that finally won the
competition with its "soft copper tent" to be
erected above the old dock of the Galärvarvet shipyard, dating from 1879.

The Vasa Museum was opened on June
15 1990.

Drawing by Studio Frank Ω Co.